MW01121233

Congrats on your New Home

by
Marianne Richmond

Congrats on your New Home

Marianne Richmond Studios, Inc.
420 N. 5th Street, Suite 840
Minneapolis, MN 55401
www.mariannerichmond.com

ISBN 0-9770000-3-6

Illustrations by Marianne Richmond

Book design by Meg Anderson

Printed in China

First Printing

Congratulations on your new home!

The place where
life's stories unfold.

May you feel
safe and happy
and cozy there!

May your home be a
favorite place to
relax, putter, and play.

Where practice
makes (almost)
perfect and hobbies
of all kinds
are accepted!

May your home
be a place
where lively
conversation
and laughter
fill the rooms...

Where disagreements
can be worked out.

And where tears
find a gentle hug.

May visitors find kindness
and hospitality overflowing...

and a spare toothbrush
if they need it!

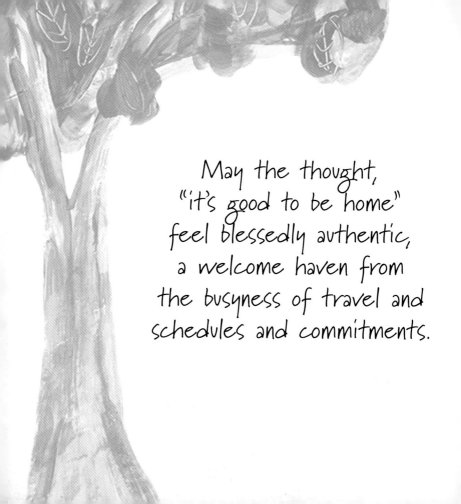

May the thought,
"it's good to be home"
feel blessedly authentic,
a welcome haven from
the busyness of travel and
schedules and commitments.

May each room eventually
tell a tale of living...

from favorite furniture

to stubborn carpet stains

to dings in the wall.

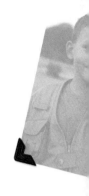

May photos and keepsakes remind you

of who and what's important.

Congratulations on your new home...

a place where memories
are created and recollected...
and treasured.

May your home
be host to simple
accomplishments
and big celebrations
of every kind!

May traditions be born
around the dinner table,
on holiday mornings,
or through the inside jokes
of those who dwell within.

May your yard be a place
for playing, relaxing, and
watching the world go by.

May your lawn
grow more flowers
than dandelions.

May you bid each day
goodbye with a feeling of
safety, security and contentment.

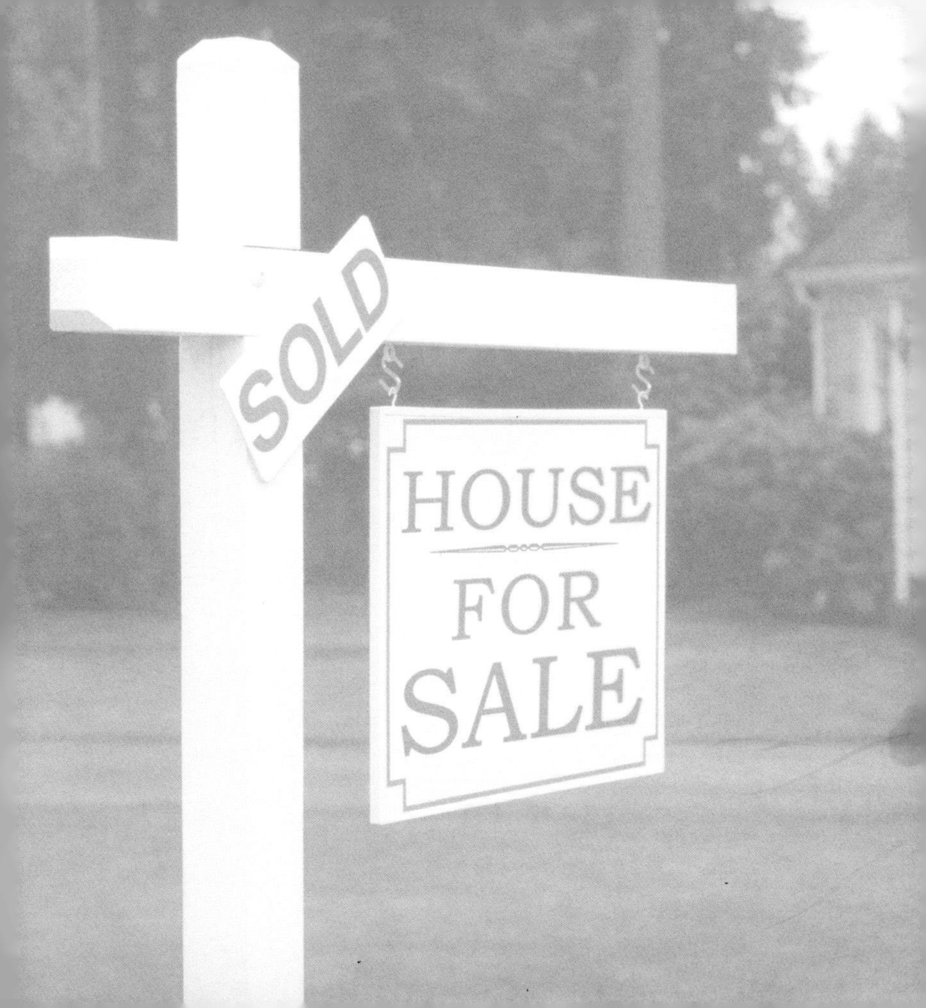
SOLD
HOUSE
FOR
SALE

Congratulations
on your new home.

May love live with you always.

A gifted author and artist, Marianne Richmond shares
her creations with millions of people worldwide
through her delightful books, cards, and giftware.
In addition to the *Simply Said...* and *Smartly Said...*
gift book series, she has written and illustrated five
additional books: **The Gift of an Angel,
The Gift of a Memory, Hooray for You!,
The Gifts of Being Grand** and **I Love You So...**

To learn more about Marianne's products, please visit
www.mariannerichmond.com.